ALSO BY SANDRA MARCHETTI

Full-length Collection:
Confluence

Chapbooks:
Sight Lines
Heart Radicals
A Detail in the Landscape
The Canopy

AISLE 228

AISLE 228

poems

SANDRA MARCHETTI

STEPHEN F. AUSTIN STATE UNIVERSITY PRESS

For more information:
Stephen F. Austin State University Press
P.O. Box 13007 SFA Station
Nacogdoches, Texas 75962
sfapress@sfasu.edu

Managing Editor: Kimberly Verhines
Editorial Assistant: Meredith Janning
Cover Art: Danny Rockett
Cover Design: Brian Mihok
Distributed by Texas A&M Consortium

ISBN: 978-1-62288-955-6

for my father, who taught me the strike zone

"How can you not be romantic about baseball?"

Moneyball

CONTENTS

Winners

ACKNOWLEDGMENTS

I give my gratitude to the editors and staffs of the following publications, in which these poems—sometimes in different versions—previously appeared:

The Account: "Late October"

Atticus Review: "Spring," "Rookie"

Baseball Prospectus: "Driving Through the Foothills of Western Pennsylvania," "Myth," "1060 W. Addison"

Blackbird: "1965," "Denouement," "Distortion"

Bone Bouquet: "Invasive," "Threshold"

Boog City: "Elysian Park"

Cobalt: "Field in Winter"

Connotation Press: "Over Sheffield Avenue"

Escape into Life: "Being a Cub Fan," "Immortality," "Tell"

The Hardball Times: "Inning Ending Twin Killing," "*The 2016 Chicago Cubs...*"

Hobart: "The Unsayable," "Broadcast," "Cross Country," "AM," "Flags," "Game 3"

Louisiana Literature: "First Poem," "Arizona," "'The good Lord wants the Cubs to win.'"

The McNeese Review: "Praise"

Moon City Review: "Extras"

museum of americana: "Listening for Bob Uecker,"
"Maddux Listens to the Game on Tape,"
"Reception"

Poet Lore: "Twilight"

Reunion: The Dallas Review: "Save"

Southwest Review: "Frame"

Split Lip Magazine: "Relish"

Sport Literate: "Fable"

Stirring: "Seams"

Stymie Mag: "Pete Rose and Ichiro Meet in Baseball Heaven or at a Card Show," "A Nine-Year Old Girl Watches the 1993 World Series"

Whale Road Review: "Strikeout," "Recording"

AISLE 228

Losers

Frame

Tucked in the western grandstand imagine
Wrigley: a sliver of light, orange-green

beams gone between Golden Arches
as scoreboard plates clink in place.

The fourth inning haze filters the sun—
a yolk yawning itself undone

in the upper deck air—to curve against
each pillar, straining my gaze in Aisle 228.

My father gripes and wipes his nose
through the April game—
the team terrible again—

yet players lope over this green hill
and our minds agree to rise
and clap for them.

The Unsayable

The Chicago Cubs went 108 years between World Series championships.

If it never happened,
would we go on buying
the season tickets, scuffling
through turnstiles, slowed
at the bag check?

If it never happened,
would we split a pizza
and a pop, a bag of chips
or a beer, huddling
as we handed over the cash?

If it never happened,
would we still applaud
the blue pennant tentative
to ascend the flagpole
after a series' win?

If it never happened,
would we root on a .500
club, be pleased with less
than 200 strikeouts,
20 errors at short?

We flicker in our seats, dimly
recede, but never leave.

1965

I picture my father
in the dimmed
attic. Wind presses
the panes lightly back,
his stomach slack
to the radio
crackling innings past.

The sound of Koufax
slaps the glove; above,
the scoreboard plates
catch each frame
in their clanking.

Listening for Bob Uecker

My father thinks you can find
a signal from anywhere—

a Mets game in Cincinnati,
the Reds in Tennessee.

I tell him sometimes the mountains
curtain the call, or a semi

bleating its long, low horn,
its lights scanning the corn.

But 50,000 watts fighting
Dolly Parton or a revival

travels. When it's clear
you can hear the Dodgers

in Chicago and know a wave
arrayed in the distance

spun out its curve
to find you.

Seams

Grip this core
formed to your

hand. Your wrist
snaps elbow, arm,

whips chest and ribs
to pace the pitch's

spin and give,
to settle the grist

in the mitt's crib.

Maddux Listens to the Game on Tape

He recalls the mound
behind his eyes,

neck tilted slightly
and mouth ajar.

He floats back to hear
what caught the black,

for the scene between
himself and the catcher:

a shiver of light
his arm shuffles through.

When Uncle Mo spins,
the sigh of a career

near done, he with Wrigley,
the crowd a choir

on the tape catching,
spooling, and righting
itself again.

Praise

Clutch the railing up the steps,
shuffle to your pew. Sing
two, a third if blessed. Whisper
cathedral, then profess.

We pray, but witness a wake
most days. We slake ashes
onto the track; a loud-
speaker calls us back.

The organ keys strike three,
abide the trinity. On Sunday
dressed our best, we crowd around
the beaming green and rise as one
spirits the blue. Tell me,
what do you do at church?

Strikeout

for Kerry Wood

After each K
he whirled to say,
"got 'em again."

With a click
of the wrist,
not quite

a fist, at 20,
we thought 20
would happen again.

On the grainy
screen, a pimpled
teen sipped

from the clouds,
a sky he couldn't
find again

until his ceiling
fell in on him.

Broadcast

*Pat Hughes has served as the radio broadcaster
of the Chicago Cubs for over 25 years.*

In the stands, I twist the dial to find you.
I click the knob then dump the clothes pile.
Walking to Dairy Queen I hear your fear—
he gave it up in the ninth, alright.

The scenes your consonants round—
those ballpark sounds—scruff rough
on my skin. You dictate my stillness
and my bend. Along the network line,
you refine each strike in attempts to mend.

First Poem

I sat in the writing center after the game. I was just a kid in eighth grade; it was 1998 and the tutor complained at "emblazoned." She was unfamiliar and made me explain, but I knew it was the only word to use, the name for my entrance that night into a collective shame.

I witnessed my first night playoff game at Wrigley—
Maddux versus Wood. For the Rookie of the Year
I craned my neck only to look back at you; my
father, we wore all the coats in the world to watch
Maddux do it again—

thread the game within his fingers and find it
between two seams. We felt for our cars in the
Lane Tech dark while the Braves took off to play a
half-full stadium.

After the tutor's strain, I lost the poem, penciled only on a loose-leaf sheet. It flew from my hands over the Lake and east—the longest out I'd ever write.

In the ninth, I stared at the weather vane, the
scoreboard plates, my breath laced through the air
air and into the offseason break.

Bright above the city, next to my father and his
father flickering, I settled in as the third generation.
When it was over, I knew I was to blame.

The poem was lost. The tutor did not know where to begin. She did not know the word. Because she did not know the word, she did not know my name.

Cross Country

At 15,000 feet
and climbing,
I look down
from Seat 7A

into a suburban
swimming pool
and feel my
glasses splash.

Whenever I
fly I search
for the baseball
diamonds.

There are so many
in the Midwest
and you can
always spot them—

how the dust plumes,
how green the grass,
how there is so much
good land for them.

AM

It doesn't have to be
a ballgame for me
to feel included,
calmed to hear
a voice other than
my own. I walk
through the house,
turn them all on,
and say hello.

Save

2003 was rare
because I wasn't
with you.

I tell myself
maybe they lost
because I wasn't.

I mouthed my
"No" from a
friend's couch,

a basement
crowded with
Cub fans.

I wonder if
I'll be with you
when it happens.

Will you
drive us up
Western Avenue,

denigrate city politics,
get us to the gate
for the early bird discount?

When it happens
I may have to embody
a relief pitcher,

relieved—who points
to the sky and kisses it,
acknowledging his ghosts.

Pete Rose and Ichiro Meet in Baseball Heaven
or at a Card Show

After Hustle's laughter
wears off, their orbits
align. Ballcap to black sun-
glasses, criminalized
and sainted, inscrutable.
God watches their gaze
settle up the middle.

Inning Ending Twin Killing

for Pat Hughes, after Elizabeth Bishop's "Poem"

What a thing
it is to listen
to you describe
grounding into
a double play.
"Two looks…
turned into
each other,"
the equivalent
of Bishop's
inherited Bristol
board. Down
7-0, this is
what "we get
for free—"
your voice
for a last
half inning.

Sunday Night

It was packed
at Wrigley the night
Glavine won his 300th.

We were losing bad
to his Mets
for most of it;

Maybe that's why
you didn't want
to applaud when

he waved to the crowd,
relieved, Cub fans
cheering him easily.

Like most, I have
second favorites,
and thirds, guys

to root for in October.
But you wouldn't
stand for history.

Driving Through the Foothills of Western Pennsylvania

I've listened to three games tonight
and don't know where my head is.

Meaningless teams chew the miles
between losing and lost.

Headlights billow up dark branches;
it is always the bottom of the ninth.

Suspending no from yes, the pitcher
finally shakes his catcher.

In the only game I see,
the score never changes.

Reception

for the 2008 NL Division Series

When my father called from the park I could
        barely hear, "Dempster's losing it out there."

I walked to my car on the street
        and pines cued up the signal.

The neighborhood cut a band
        in the Virginia sky, but static

clustered my sunroof, circled
        out from the wringing of my hands.

Already behind we couldn't find a hit—
        winning 97 gone with a fiddling of the dial.

From the mound you shook off Soto's sign,
        the announcer said, and instead

of finishing them, the walks fell
        like stars from your hand.

Denouement

Beer on the bricks and cheap meat—
piss that brines the seats
and the frame as we exit
the park at the end of the game.

A dozen doors thwack open
dull as scrapped cups.
Through the clatter, a popcorn vendor
crams his bags in the trash.

We meet in a square
of air below the stairs
to curse and bless,
sopped with sweat.

Hands grimed on tunnel walls,
slathered in mustard and ads,
shuffle us from the cube in sun,
ants pressed away from the day.

Over Sheffield Avenue
after John Thorn

I'm playing baseball in the Garden of Eden.
Scratch that. I'm writing baseball
in the Garden of Eden—where old cars
ride street corner curves in our square
city, while vendors hawk peanuts.

I'm writing baseball out of the Garden of Eden.
Clouds sail the blue-gold lake, a tincture
Titian never mastered. Players skim
the surface grass in pinstriped cottons:
blue hats, blue socks, blue numbers.

I'm writing baseball out of the Garden.
I touch the field to liquefy it—
a prism painted deftly on my eye.
I'm writing baseball as it never was,
from a Sunday on which we won it all.

Winners

Twilight

Some young men play catch
in a field, call each other
on balls and strikes. How
can they possibly know? Dancing
through the grass, one high,
then low, and up again—
just outside! The seams slap
old leather. How can we know
where the strike zone is—imaginary
cube, filament I could not hold
in my hand? I asked, "How can
you tell?" and my father said,
"Watch—you'll learn. You'll know."
They play, rhythmic and swift,
until the young men are gone.

Myth
for Ichiro

You know
part of it is
him rising from
the Sea of Japan
again, a siren
who whispers, *never*
die. We want to believe
in permanence, the not
quite going, the falling
back into the waves
and surfacing spring
after spring, walking
the sand in his cleats.

Spring

"Like a blind man at the ballgame, I need a radio."

~Annie Dillard

I'm falling asleep to your voice today.
It's 80 degrees in Mesa and blue
skies color your radio play
as wind whips my picture window.

The camelback couch creaks when I lift
my head to listen to a play: Soler
throws out a runner at third—you say,
"Few outfielders can do that today."

I lie back into the crackling AM sway;
when I wake we've lost and into the news
you've gone for the day.

Rookie

He scuffs his spike
in the dirt, staring
down the glove.

How odd it seems,
this child uneasy
as 35,000 look on.

The woman nods,
knows how he walks,
open, toward her.

Extras

It was late when I walked by the sushi place.
Through the picture window, I saw a man and
his son, the owners perhaps, sitting beneath an
anticipatory glow. They were watching the
ballgame in the dark dining room. So unlike
you and me, these silent men resting after
restaurant work, faithful through extra innings.
I had flipped off the car radio, but I remember
now we won. It was their reward for not going
home, for waiting on the pitcher to throw.

Being a Cub Fan

How many
minutes
of my life
have I spent
with hands
clasped,
hoping for one
to go out?

Recording
for the 2015 NL Division Series clincher

As Harry Caray sings
the seventh inning stretch
I grieve, my hands pour
toward the grainy signal
filling our living room.
My father is at the game
and is so tired of hearing
this song, its lament.

I whisper
to him: *it's over,*
it's almost over,
and since I want
to believe, I wipe
my cheek.

Field in Winter

Snow lights on the mound
and settles downy as wings.

Slicked in spit turned
ice, the concave

diamond spreads
against night:

a shallow bowl filled
quick to white—

the stadium a breath
flared then folded tight.

Fable

My mother's parents met in Brooklyn, and I wear
my grandmother's stone. I'm sure her diamond
reflected Ebbets with him in tow, the severe man
who gifted its glow.

I imagine them gliding past the gates, him admiring
her tiny waist. He'd say to their children, "dessert
is a look at your mother"—just a taste.

I must begin at the luncheonettes though, before
Jackie slid into home. They made dates to rip
tickets and she'd smile while he snickered. My
grandparents headed west after the Dodgers left,
Ebbets sold and blown.

Arizona

Down the first base line,
I saw your body stretched
like an A on the mound,
your right arm a slash
line across it.

A spring training game
in mid-March, you only
threw a few innings, but I
could tell your pitches
were up without replay.

In the crowd I hid among
the retirees. White men
with white hair in white
shirts holding scorecards and I
thought about asking,

What is it like for your team
to leave you, as this team will
leave in a couple of weeks
for a city at work that no longer
stops its afternoons for baseball?

Immortality

for the left-handed pitcher

He pointed
to me
and said:
never
underestimate
a veteran
who might
have a little
magic left.

Relish

My teeth break
the casing, all
vinegar and salt;

I swallow the sweet
bread, the ball-
park's steam.

Pans of hot
water, mustard
on plates—grated

onions, please—
America's game,
feed me.

Invasive

The mallard lay
in short center
field and no one,
not even the ump,
came close to her
grass. Russell ranged
to his left but behind
her, another body
for the baseball
to dodge.

Distortion

I won't forget listening
to a Brewers game
as the sun sunk over
the jack pine ridges
of the Upper Peninsula.
The signal glowed
fainter with each ray
disappearing. I was
northing with Bob Uecker
and when the light
dimmed well past nine,
Milwaukee was losing
and so was I, winking
slow across the shoreline,
my ears wrecked in the static
of a bobblehead giveaway.

The 2016 Chicago Cubs led MLB in DER (Defensive Efficiency Rating) and some consider them the greatest defensive team of all time.

Snatched from its trajectory—
the catch hauled
and slung.

Hands work the blur.

A balance picked,
juggled, with one
flick—sunk.

Have you seen a net before?
The web of the glove
is what it was.

Elysian Park
for the 2016 NL Championship Series

The ballclub parades into Chavez Ravine
natty as a marching band. Pressed uniforms
catch the Santa Anas and ripple in the jet stream.
The spirits trail behind. Down Vin Scully
Avenue their cleats clack and gleam.

Flags

In 2016, the Chicago Cubs won the National League pennant.
In 2015, the Kansas City Royals won the American League pennant.

Today I clicked
on the car radio in Chicago
and the sports hosts exhaled

in a shout, "I knew we'd do it!
Was there ever any doubt?"
I wiped the sleep from my eyes
and breathed, driving along
the tree-lined street.

Last October 22nd, I drove
to Kansas City and was there
when the Royals won the pennant.
The town exhaled with clout.
Radio hosts said,
"There was never any doubt."

During the game I steered
past Kauffman Stadium
on the longest road in the state.
Between the tree-lined curves
I heard the hometown call,
the broadcasters clearly stirred.

Light standards glowed through
the clouds as cars passed.
I felt serene, as if it were
my team.

A Nine-Year Old Girl Watches the 1993 World Series

That square of unimaginable
green, his leap over a cloud.

Out of a red cap, curls
tumbled with sweat beads.

Color patches beamed from
the box in our toyroom;
I craned my neck to see joy—

Late October

It's the first night of the World Series
and ten jets, like stars, home
toward O'Hare. Runways roll
out the plains in draped carpet.
Even though little league is over,
each ballfield lit up as if
by candles at the dinner table,
welcoming someone's return.

Game 3

for the 2016 World Series

I kissed my father's cheek for good
luck in the firehouse driveway.
We were 27 outs away from a Series
lead when he entered through Gate K.

I took my seat on the Waveland curb
and relayed Pat's play-by-play
to guys in lawn chairs sucking booze
through the scoreless game. Grandmothers,
perched as finches, waited on my radio's say.

The intersection bled into the ballpark's
glow. From the streets below, we held
the diamond aloft on our exhales alone.

Tell

The '98
Yankees
are still
the best
team I've
ever seen.

Don't you
know how
easy it is
to fault
the one
you love?

Threshold

for the 2016 World Series clincher

"The ball sailed a bit,"
Rizzo paused, "but it
went in my glove."

When it landed
in his mitt, Hughes
cried, "It's in time!"

His voice cracking
over first base,
dying beneath

Martinez's cleat.
Silence—then
a bursting beat.

"The good Lord wants the Cubs to win."
~Harry Caray

I dreamt you rewound
the last play that evening
our fortunes changed
and took it away.

In the nightmare you
lead the trophy back
from our owner's hands
to the commissioner's grasp.

Then Bryant slipped
and missed the ball,
his smile twisted
to torture. Or maybe

he threw but the seams
popped loose from Rizzo's
mitt—two on, two out.
Either way, you shifted

it from our grasp
and settled its heft
back onto your lap.

1060 W. Addison

Our childhoods hang
like ghosts in the aisles
waiting on us
to ascend the stairs,
snatch, and wear them.

Little haunt, this
was the first heart
break we knew.
We breathe the air
and are gone.

INTERVIEW WITH SANDRA MARCHETTI
ON THE PUBLICATION OF *Aisle 228*

Kimberly Verhines: What was your process of developing the poems for *Aisle 228?* Walk us through your writing process.

Sandra Marchetti: Even before I finished my first book, *Confluence,* I knew this was the project that I wanted to tackle next. I already had an idea of the book and some of the poems, but something inside of me wouldn't let me write it until that first collection had found a publisher. This was that rare occurrence where, as a writer, you know you have an idea for a book in you before it begins. Of course, I couldn't know that in the process of writing this book the Cubs would win the World Series (about three years into the eight-year long process!). I knew I wanted to write about games I heard stories of, attended, and listened to on the radio. So, I started there. But the book was going to be about more than the Cubs—about the game itself and how we consume it—so I wrote poems about how baseball enlivens our five senses and about historical markers in the game's history intertwined with my family history. It is a selective and chronological history.

KV: Who were your favorite authors and poets to read growing up? How would you say they influenced your writing?

SM: I was in a performance group in elementary school that gave dramatic readings of poems, and it impacted me greatly. We read Shel Silverstein, "Jabberwocky," and others in front of live audiences, and two of the baseball poems we performed were "Baseball's Sad Lexicon" ("Tinkers to Evers to Chance") and "Casey at the Bat." So, that was certainly influential. In college, I really fell in love with Sharon Olds and then her confessional predecessors. Today, Elizabeth Bishop, Li-Young Lee, Octavio Paz, and Carl Phillips most influence me. Also, I love the baseball writing of Andrew Forbes, Jason Koo, and Annie Dillard. But, the voices of the game are those who inspired the cadence of this collection: Vin Scully, Pat Hughes, Len Kasper, Bob Uecker.

KV: What significance does the title of the collection, *Aisle 228*, carry?

SM: *Aisle 228* was the section where my father and I sat at Wrigley Field through all of the "lean" years—when the team was bad or almost good enough. He bought tickets from a season ticket holder whom he worked with, and the guy sold them just as the team was starting to win again—after the 2014 season. My father told him it was a big mistake, but he didn't listen! We sit on the other side of the ballpark now, but those seats were a front row to Eden—the lighting, the angles, the view—it was perfect, even with all the losing. The first half of the book is written from the perspective of those seats, directly behind first base, down the right field line in the box seats.

KV: What about the significance of the poems in the "Losers" section as compared to the "Winners" section? How did you decide how to organize the collection?

SM: The "Losers" section is what defined us as Cub fans for over 100 years! So, it's significant. Cub fans wore that melancholy earned from steady losing like a badge of honor. With "Winners" and "Losers," I almost wanted to give the readers a mental break just by looking at the Table of Contents—a sort of—"ok, this is going to have a happy ending." Cub fans really can't take another Rajai Davis moment! I decided to order the collection pretty sequentially, despite some advice from a well-respected author and friend to do something different. Perhaps due to my lack of creativity, I couldn't see it any other way. I wanted to travel along the timeline of this team for the last 60 years—with other memories interspersed as well, of course.

KV: So, it's safe to assume you're a Cubs fan? Is that because of being in or around Chicago or is there another reason? Are there any other teams you favor?

SM: Yes, it's safe to assume that! I love Chicagoland—I went down the career path I did partially because I wanted to move back home after grad school and keep going to lots of ballgames every summer—I just couldn't give that up. In "First Poem," I mention, "the third generation" and I am a third-generation fan—I do remember faintly watching the Cubs on my grandfather's old TV at his house when I was very, very young. They lived on the north side of the city and that's where my father grew up, going to games himself as a kid. I'm sure I couldn't walk the first time I went to Wrigley Field. There are other teams (and individual players) I temporarily root for—I think it's something Cub fans adopted when our team regularly missed the playoffs. I definitely root for history to be made. I talk about it in "Sunday Night"—my father and I were present at Tom Glavine's 300th career win—a game that took place at Wrigley on Sunday Night Baseball. I was awed.

KV: Your collection is dedicated to your father, and the poems centering around attending baseball games with him gives the book the feeling of a memoir. Despite this being a poetry collection, would you consider it a memoir in any way? Why or why not?

SM: I would, but perhaps like we might say about some translations—it's impressionistic. I always tell folks who ask me about my writing, and myself as a character in it, that "poets can lie too." That's not just a trick up the fiction writer's sleeve! Maybe readers don't think about it since poetry is housed with the nonfiction in the Dewey Decimal System? There are poems in this book, like "1965" and "Fable" that are retellings of stories I heard once, where I had to imagine what really happened. I enjoyed doing that, and making those tales a bit larger than life.

KV: The epigraph from the film *Moneyball* asks about being romantic about baseball. What does it mean to you to be romantic about baseball?

SM: I think it's really important when you are talking about baseball and poetry to let yourself as the reader—and the writer—give into that nostalgia we have for the game. Baseball is a game of poetry, symmetry, and myth. To resist that is unhelpful, or at least it was to me. As poets, we are always told to avoid sentimentality. But, I didn't feel that was productive for this book. I had to reach into all the memories and make some beauty even from the painful ones. And the beauty of baseball isn't always classical either—sure there are the crisp uniforms and the blue skies, but I think of the piss and beer smell at the ballpark as romantic too, and the dirt falling out of the players' belt buckles after a slide.

KV: Is there a poem in the collection that you consider a personal favorite? Why or why not?

SM: If you can believe it, "Frame" and "Denouement" were drafted as one poem. I liked the light/dark effect they created together but decided there was more to explore, so I separated them. Still, they are probably personal favorites. Willard Spiegelman, the venerable and now-retired editor at *The Southwest Review* picked "Frame" out of the slush pile to publish soon after I started the project, and that gave me confidence to continue. I thought, maybe there are some poetry readers who are baseball fans! And it turned out to be true, and also there are many baseball fans who like these poems—so that was a real boost. "Distortion" is also a personal favorite.

KV: In the poem titled "Praise," you compare attending a ballgame to being at church. Is there a spiritual side to your love of baseball? Or, how does religion fit into your experiences with baseball as a whole?

SM: The idea of coming together as a crowd or "congregation" to take part in something bigger than yourself—to watch for miracles and pray for them—is a common denominator. We sing at the ballpark, we experience awe and grace, we queue up for our blessings. Baseball is also quite akin to Christianity—it's a game of threes and symmetry, and could easily conjure up the trinity. We wear special clothes when we enter "cathedrals." Baseball is also our oldest game, full of legends and sacred icons. I grew up in a religious tradition, so for me, the connections were easy to find. I don't think you have to be religious to appreciate the game, but the game will bring out the spiritual and superstitious side in you!

KV: Do you think there is a particular poem in the collection that could be seen as the climax? Or, in other words, is there a poem that is built up to and serves as the shining moment?

SM: "Threshold" is the climactic poem. The Cubs definitively win the World Series in that moment. I wanted to make sure the poem included the voices of that moment's central players—among them first baseman Anthony Rizzo and Pat Hughes, the Cubs' radio play-by-play broadcaster—since they were living it right alongside the rest of us, trying to make sense of it. So, the book has a really slow build, considering "Threshold" is the third-to-last piece.

KV: What is your earliest memory associated with baseball? How has it influenced you both in life and in writing the collection?

SM: I remember being very small, sitting in the very last row in the upper deck at Wrigley, up against the fencing covering the back of the grandstand. I was scared I would fall out of the back of the ballpark and into the street. My earliest day-to-day memories of the game are probably best encapsulated in the poem, "A Nine-Year Old Girl Watches the 1993 World Series." We watched so many games in our den (affectionately called the "toyroom") while I played with Barbie dolls. I remember the colors, the sounds, and the thrill of that World Series. When Annie Dillard talks about children seeing "color patches" she was talking about me in that moment. I could feel the sweat pouring off Mitch Williams' hair. And this was before HD!

KV: In "Fable," you describe the role of baseball in the love between your mother's parents, and how you continue to uphold their memories. How does baseball fit into that, both literally and figuratively? Will it, or how will it, continue to play a role in your life and in future generations?

SM: Baseball definitely plays an important role in my life. When you live in the Chicago area, you need something to look forward to. Right now, we're picking out the tickets for the games we'll start attending from April to September this year. That's motivation in January. Baseball has become something of a niche sport. It's not so easy to bet on, and it's mostly non-contact, plus it's measured, so it's lost some traction in our society. Also, when streaming games, the blackout restrictions don't help. Some of these new rule changes—including a pitch clock—will be helpful in drawing in bigger audiences. However, the way to get folks interested in baseball is to bring them to a game. It doesn't have to be an MLB contest—minor league baseball is so much fun. Once you go, you'll want to return—I promise. Minor league games are the one place where I never want to pick up my phone because there's just such a sensory feast in every second.

KV: What has the overall experience of writing and building this collection been like for you? How has it been the same and /or different from the books you've published previously?

SM: I labored over my first full-length collection and thought it took a long time to write and publish—five years. This one was a whole different beast. I wrote, revised, and submitted *Aisle 228* for eight years. Most of the poems were done after about five years or so, but the revisions were painstaking, and I would add or subtract one piece at a time. The collection got close to publication at several presses, which was an incentive to keep going. Trade publishers liked the idea of the collection but didn't know how to market it. My dream was to work with a university press and after reading some of SFA Press' poetry, I submitted. It was the perfect match! I was mostly relieved—to be honest—that the book would finally see the light of day.

KV: What do you hope readers will take away from *Aisle 228* after reading? Is there something in particular you hope will stick out to them?

SM: For the baseball fans—this book is a love letter to our game. For the poets—baseball is just a metaphor for everything else important in life. I'm joking! No, I want the collection to be about awe, terror, and beauty. It may not be so fashionable these days, but those are the things I explore in my work, and I want the book to live in those moments.

KV: Is there anything else you would like to add?

SM: This quote from *A League of Their Own* where Jimmy Duggan is talking to Dottie Henson at the end of the movie about why she "retired" from the game has been on my mind a lot lately, and I was reminded of it when writing the collection, too: "It's supposed to be hard. If it wasn't hard, everyone would do it. The hard is what makes it great."

ABOUT THE AUTHOR

SANDRA MARCHETTI is the author of *Confluence*, a full-length collection of poetry from Sundress Publications (2015). She is also the author of four chapbooks of poetry and lyric essays, including *Sight Lines* (Speaking of Marvels Press, 2016), *Heart Radicals* (ELJ Publications, 2015), *A Detail in the Landscape* (Eating Dog Press, 2014), and *The Canopy* (MWC Press, 2012). Sandra's poetry appears widely in *Blackbird, Baseball Prospectus, FanGraphs, Southwest Review, Poet Lore,* and elsewhere. Her essays can be found at *The Rumpus, Pleiades, Mid-American Review, Barrelhouse, Fansided,* and other venues. Sandy is the Poetry Editor Emerita at *River Styx* Magazine. She earned an MFA in Creative Writing—Poetry from George Mason University and now serves as the Coordinator of Tutoring Services at the College of DuPage in the Chicagoland area.

CPSIA information can be obtained
at www.ICGtesting.com
Printed in the USA
JSHW021650110423
40198JS00003B/14

9 781622 889556